To Sue + Mark
with love + light

Heart Balm

WHISPERS AND WORD POTIONS

JO DYER

Cover image by: Romana Bovan based on an
original illustration by Emet Aron
Heart Balm vine illustrations by: Emet Aron
Book design by: SWATT Books Ltd

Printed in the United Kingdom
First Printing, 2021

ISBN: 978-1-7398624-0-4 (Hardback)
ISBN: 978-1-7398624-1-1 (eBook)

Jo Dyer
Belper, Derbyshire

Contents

Heart Balm

Oh! how I have needed that quietness of late.
That cherished space
where I can see and feel the spaciousness of the stars.
A place of home-coming
where the lightness of the Linden Blossom resides.
Where I am warmed
by the late autumn glowing embers
spread before me.

Oh! how I have needed that tenderness of late.
The gentle touch
of my heart cradled amongst steadfast trees.
The embrace of nature;
Her soothing balm in the breeze
and under my feet.
My Soul held with compassion
as I find my way back to myself.

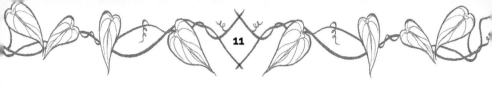

Whispers and Word Potions

Welcome to this book of Whispers and Word Potions. Thank you for opening it.

I wonder if poetry is about to enter your being for the first time or whether it discovered you a while back.

Poetry discovered me when I was a small child.

My mum used to take us to a wonderful bookshop. It was like a cave; below street level, down some mysterious steps near the Cathedral in the City where I was born. It wasn't a place you would venture into without your mum! Inside, the walls were dark wooden panels and the atmosphere was one of sacred reverence. The books were portals to another world.

One day I picked up a large book called Hilda Boswell's Treasury of Poetry. It was the illustrations that caught my eye – colourful, warm, inviting. I opened the book at the first poem and was immediately, entranced.

I found this book under our Christmas tree that year and on Sunday family gatherings that winter, I would read the poems out loud to my Nan, my Uncle and the rest of my immediate family. Poetry had entered my heart and there it made its home. I was 6 years old.

The next summer, my dad bought me another book of poetry – The Child's Garden of Verses by Robert Louis Stevenson. In reading this book, I discovered some critical abilities. I didn't like all of the poems, but there was one that I loved and which I still read occasionally. It is called Escape at Bedtime.

> "The lights from the parlour and kitchen
> Shone out
> Through the blinds and the windows and
> Bars;
> And high overhead and all moving about
> There were thousands of millions of stars".

It ends with:

> "They saw me at last, and they chased me with
> cries,
> And they soon had me packed into bed;
> But the glory kept shining and bright in my
> Eyes,
> And the stars going round in my head".

This poem still evokes a sense of expansiveness and possibility in me to this day.

I wrote my first poem when I was 11 during my first year at Grammar School. You'll find the poem in this book. It's called Christ an Imposter. I wrote it, knowing it would shock my teacher. I almost *didn't* write it – I thought there might be 'consequences' for writing something that would be seen as 'controversial'. I'm so glad I did and here's why – it enabled me to express something that I was afraid to speak out loud. It enabled me to take a risk that I would never have taken otherwise.

In allowing my imagination to explore the question I was curious about (what was said at Christ's trial?), I connected with something deep within me – an imagination that I hadn't known was there.

Gosh – that was a long time ago and even though, at that time, I didn't go on to embark upon a poetic odyssey, making poetry a major part of my life, I think I can say with honesty, that I was changed in some way – permanently. It was the first time I had given myself permission to speak; I overcame fear and stepped outside my comfort zone. For some reason, I speculated, I would be ok because it was a poem.

It has taken me over 50 years to learn the thing about poetry that I want to share with you. You might already know this but the weight and power of it have only recently come into *my* awareness.

This is it: – that experiencing poetry connects us to parts of our being that lay hidden, unexpressed and possibly even unknown to us. The forgotten wounds, delights, pain, unresolved, knotty issues have a light turned onto them and we experience them anew, or for the first time. We *witness ourselves* and from here, we grow.

When we allow a poem to enter our energy, we are changed. We experience ourselves more fully; more completely. The poem helps us to step into our fullness. It is a home coming.

Poetry is not alone in this, of course. Other forms of writing (a good book), music, sculpture, art, immersion in nature, these all have a similar impact. Poetry however, has the power, I feel, to bring this experience into sharp focus very quickly. There is something about the precision and economy of the carefully chosen words that hit home with a deep impact.

It was this growing awareness that led me to write 'word potions' for my Vibrational Essence clients. I am a vibrational essence practitioner. For those of you unfamiliar with this, vibrational essences are water that contains the energetic imprint of a flower, a crystal or any other energetic entity or place, (For example, I make essences with Moon energy as well as with flowers). They work to raise our energetic vibration and to bring our energetic system into balance, enabling us to connect with our centre and deep wisdom. From here we are able to live our days in a more easeful and present way and bring about subtle, yet transformational shifts in emotional states and ultimately behaviour and our experience of the world.

Word Potions are poems that embody the energy of the intentions for transformation contained in the work myself and my clients are doing together and in the essence combinations I make up for them. These poems amplify the energy of change but they also help the recipient to shine a light on the issues they want to work with. You will find a few examples in the pages that follow.

The 'Whispers' are the voices of nature; of trees, flowers and non-human creatures of planet Earth. I started to feel these whispers when I worked as a professional gardener, tending 14 acres of organic gardens. I sensed that they had stories to tell me, they had something to say. Often, a question would form itself in my consciousness and I wrote the answers as poems. One day, I realised that these 'whispers' would form the basis of a collection of poems that I would publish. Here they are.

The flowers and trees have entrusted their stories to me – the depth, the pain and the joy of them and I have given them a voice for they too need to be heard and witnessed. They too are kindred Souls that need compassionate witnessing. They have so much to tell us; so much to offer us.

The poems in this book then, speak to the human need for connection, belonging, validation, acceptance and love and for the need to express these and have them met. When these needs are unmet, we suffer – our tender heart receives a blow and is bruised. This bruising begins from the moment we are born. Our response is often to armour ourselves, close our heart and protect ourselves the best we can. We are all required at some point in our lives to connect with our inner warrior; to hear the call to arms for self-survival. We often forget at these times, that our most potent weapon is the love that lives in our heart. It is only by expressing and witnessing our pain that we can open our heart and let that love come forth to do its work.

So, this is a book for anyone who endures the pain of a bruised heart – which is, in fact, every single one of us. These poems represent the compassionate witnessing of anger, loneliness, grief – the myriad bruises our tender hearts endure. There is tragedy and comedy but most of all there is the need to be heard and the need to say what must be said. They contain within the affirmations we all long to hear – that you are loved, you are whole, you are enough; you are heard and witnessed, you are not alone *and you matter.*

Let these poems be a balm for the heart.

"For poems are not words, after all, but fires for the cold, ropes let down to the lost, something as necessary as bread in the pockets of the hungry. Yes, indeed."

(Mary Oliver A Poetry Handbook 1994 p122).

A Bruised Heart

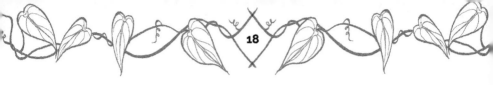

A Bruised Heart

What a strange and confusing thing it is
to be told that we have sinned
so profoundly, so fundamentally
that we need a God to save us.

My Soul rises up in rebellion.
How dare they lie and deceive
such a tender young heart?
No, worse – lay shame at my door.

Was that the moment when the seed of doubt was planted?
Or perhaps there were too many to recall.
As children we are so vulnerable
and have yet to learn compassion
or discernment;
and so, our seedling hearts are bruised so easily.

Bruise upon bruise, upon bruise.
Each one posing a question
we are ill-equipped to answer.
And so, we choose our weapons;
clothe ourselves with armour
and prepare to fight.
Because it's a rare thing
for our pleas for compassionate witnessing
to be honoured.

Fancy Dress

Shame is such a terrible thing
to inflict upon a child.
Haven't we all been put to its sword?
That all-consuming feeling of annihilation;
Disempowerment and bewilderment;
World turned upside downment.
Nothing is what it seemed to be.

One routine day at school.
One of those days when you are given the chance to show
your Mum how much you love her.
The creation of a gift borne from the
germinating seeds of creativity.

I dared to accept the invitation to take those first steps
into the adventure of self-expression.
My innocent child's Soul leapt joyfully to the challenge;
Lost in colours, shapes and love,
my hands were guided by my heart.

Wrenched away from my mindful artistry,
The teacher's booming anger raged,
"Real flowers don't look like that you stupid child!"

One routine day at school turned into a crucifixion.
In an instant I am wearing a crown of thorns,
when only moments before my hair was adorned with daisies
and I was a Goddess.
I shrink in shock and confusion as I'm accused
of heinous crimes against the plant world.

I wonder at how impoverished one's view of the world must be
when a child, creating something from her heart
can induce such vitriol.

My flower was just in fancy dress.

Pendulus Beech
- A Gentleman Residing
in Derbyshire

I could've been magnificent too.
Was meant to be
but they planted others so close
I couldn't breathe.

I could've been the star turn.
Was never meant to be,
They made sure of that.

Have you seen my brother over there?
The first born.
Given all the space he needed.
In full view of every passer-by.
Given carte blanche.
A comforting arm for the grieving widows.
A warm embrace for bereft, despairing mothers
torn asunder by loss so unfathomable
there are no words
only anguished lines and hollowed out eyes.

I've longed to play my part too.
I've reached out to so many lost souls.
But every time I get so far
they cut me back,
Mutilate me.
My grotesque stumps and misshapen limbs
bear witness to the butchery I've endured.

I could've been magnificent too
except for the fact that I'm just in the wrong place.
Jostling for position,
I have to make the best of a bad job.

Have you seen my brother over there?
The first born.
The golden boy; lording it.
Given all the light he needed.
Given pride of place.
Guaranteed a place in the history books.
Spared the paralysing terror of the chainsaw.

And I'm afforded no such reverence.
I see the quizzical looks and recoiling faces.
The sour taste my contorted form produces in mouths
too polite to spit out the truth of what they see.

And you need to ask me why I'm so bitter?

HEART BALM BY JO DYER

Thrift

I hope you know how lucky you are
Princess.
Sitting on your throne up there
basking in the sunshine;
enjoying the best of everything.
Embraced by warming stone;
Untested by winter frosts or brutal winds.

I doubt you've ever given it a moment's thought
the way the Stars and Planets aligned
to put you where you are
and me, where I am.

You are so beautiful, so vital,
You shine.
I envy you the way you can hold up your head
so confidently.
You are an affirmation.

I wonder if you can see me
down here
clinging on for dear life.
Every day a question mark that brings
my existence into doubt.
Can you even begin to imagine how tenuous my
hold on life is?
I am defined by vulnerability.
I am so small, so insignificant, so unnecessary.

I hope you know how much I admire you
Warrior.
Your soul laid bare down there.
Braving the worst an unforgiving world
throws at you.
Suffering what seems to be an endless hell
amongst the tyranny of a merciless storm.
I wonder if you've ever given it a moment's thought
the way the stars and planets aligned
to put you where you are
and me, where I am.

You are so steadfast, so resilient.
You endure.
I envy you your courage and fortitude in the face
of all your trials.
You are an affirmation.

I wonder if you have noticed me
Up here
Living a charmed life of warmth and safety.
Shielded from any form of potential calamity
save a particularly hot, dry summer.
Can you even begin to imagine how stifling my existence feels?
How much I long to have my world shaken?
I am defined by shame.
I am so small, so insignificant, so unnecessary.

TeaSel

I know I make you feel uncomfortable.
I'm the fly in the ointment;
The wrong shade of whatever it is
that doesn't go with your shoes.
Your faces give the game away.
The less inhibited openly display revulsion.
The more polite just avert their eyes.
But it's the silence that's the hardest thing to bear.

It comes suddenly
but I always know it's coming.
Ten metres either side and all is sweetness and light;
Smiles and an easiness of movement and expression.
Joyful chatter, shared appreciation,
Admiration.
The cameras might even click.

Five metres either side and eyes begin to search
for something else to look at.
My immediate neighbours are suddenly much more interesting,
Beguiling;
Bigged up by your over compensation.
You suddenly feel compelled to invade their space;
Thrusting your face into theirs.
They squirm against
uninvited and unwelcome stroking and caressing with clumsy fingers.

You might stop to confirm your disapproval
with easy-to-read non-verbals,
but most often you hasten past
eyes fixed upon the next be-dazzling object;
The next beauty whose imperfections now
go unnoticed.

Mine are on full display.

Too tall, too gangly, too plain, too prickly,
too common.
I know what I am.
You could at least do me the honour of acknowledging it to my face.

An Angry Heart

Blackthorn

The time is here once more
when the light seems lighter
and the air flows more freely through grasses that suddenly
seem longer and greener.
We tremble as we offer up our gifts to you
because we know what is to come.
And yet, we give.
It is our purpose.

Why do you mis-use us and abuse us,
persecute and destroy us
when what we offer you comes from a place of love
and is freely given?

No strings,
No agenda,
No price attached.

You come for us with hearts full of fear and hate;
with minds that cannot understand,
to butcher and defile, eradicate and
annihilate us.

Have you forgotten that we are your mothers,
your sisters;
Daughters?
Do you not see the purity of our intention?
Do you not feel the joy we feel in easing your pain?
Do you not know the love that fills our hearts?

Yes, we are afraid.
We fear you.
But know this.
When you come for us, we will fight.
We are stronger and more powerful than you know.
You will feel the searing heat of flesh pierced by spears
sharpened with our determination to protect our sisters
and survive.

We long for the day when we no longer dread the return of the light.
The day when you have learned that strength can only be found in love.
And we can stand beside one another
in truth, in love, in peace.

Christ an Imposter (1972)

Ring a bell for morning mass.
Gather all the Holy folk.
For today a preacher passes through
and has come to wash away our sins.

He calls himself the son of God.
He says he is a King.
But where is his sword,
his armour, his shield and gold?

He wears no robes of silk or fur
or crown upon his head.
This man is an imposter there is no doubt.

"Crucify him! Crucify him!
if justice is to be done.

Now let him where the crown he deserves -
The crown of thorns".

Holly

And how do I feel today?

Which response is most appropriate,
most 'real'?
Which response is for public consumption
and which for private grief?

"I am a pink squidgy thing", I reply,
pleased at my creativity.
"I am slowly turning, tumbling across the universe,
Falling, spinning, squirming, writhing.
I am many shades of pink.
From cool watermelon to red hot Bloody Mary
and when you squeeze me I hurt – just a little.
Although, sometimes I am pierced to my core
and the pain is paralyzing.

Yesterday, I hardly moved at all.
I was a candy floss butterfly under scrutiny.
Today, I have long sharp spikes so watch out!
I am Paw-Paw.
But always the same soft centre –
Strawberry Fool!"

My soft centre runs like hot molten lava.
Each shift of the bubbling mass tearing at me;
Ripping apart old scars, cauterizing fresh wounds.
How can being alive produce such a seething mass of
chaotic fears and suffocating passions?

Why can't people resist the temptation to squeeze,
and prod, poke and prick soft, pink, squidgy things?
Don't they know they are playing with fire?
Don't they know that the raspberry ripple filling
they find so appetising; so delicious,
is really flesh consuming acid?

Today my veins pulsate with a stalking anger that
frightens me.
My spikes are not for my protection but for yours.
I'll let you know when it's safe to approach once more.

HEART BALM BY JO DYER

Christ The Imposter (1981)

"What is this man?
This Jesus Christ, this 'Son of God'?
King of Jews?
Bear witness to his 'finery'.
Where is his crown?
Do you see fine clothes?

RAGS!

Subjects?
He has none but a handful of wretched vagabonds
that he has seduced with his magic.
Yes, magic!
For what other evidence has he shown to prove himself?
Only petty conjuring tricks
performed upon those he has corrupted.

Will you see justice done?"

"CRUCIFY! CRUCIFY!"

"Let him wear the crown he deserves –
The crown of thorns!"

Centranthus ruber

My name is *Centranthus ruber;*
Feared and revered as a powerful God.
You should throw yourselves at my feet
in adoration and prayer.
Why then do you insult me with this deceitful confusion;
This feigned ignorance?

Whose tongue was it that started the lies?
Show him to me that I might
rain down my wrath upon him.
Bring me the fool who dared dishonour me;
The traitor whose lips were the first to mock and
insult me as they formed the word
Valerian
And coupled me with it.

Just the faintest sound of that witch's name
turns my blood to molten lava.
Valerian.
Female.
Circes of the plant world.
A pathetic, worthless, sorceress.
That simpering, whispering alchemist
whom I could swarm over,
Asphyxiate,
Annihilate
With just one ejaculation of my seed.

I will know who works to humiliate me
and they will feel the sharp spearhead of my vengeance.
Oh yes!
And Valerian, you pale-faced skinny conspirator,
You will be banished from my Kingdom for eternity.

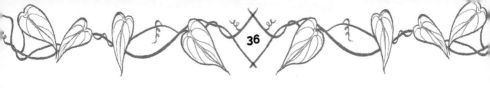

A Lonely Heart

Rose

Tea is taken at three pm
precisely.
Brewed for five minutes;
Boiling water,
carefully poured into a bone china teapot;
On the terrace if the weather in clement.
More often, in the library.
Thirty perfect minutes
snatched from the word-bound world
she inhabits.

The linen tablecloth is pressed smooth.
Sprayed with lavender water
and edged with antique lace from Nottingham.
Exquisite.
It had graced her grandmother's table
when she was a child.

The mantel clock is accurate, of course.
At ten minutes past three
five sips have been taken.
The first scone waits patiently on a plate.
The butter is still a little too cold.
It always is.

She sits upright in delicate shades of pink silk and cashmere.
Soft, quivering colours and textures
disguising steeliness, resilience
and a tendency towards hostility.
The pearls that complete the deception
were a gift from her mother
on the day of her wedding.
She blinks and recoils slightly
as she remembers the excuses.

Three seconds of anger.
Two of regret.
One of forgiveness.
Spilt milk should never be a cause for tears.
At three thirty,
tea has been taken.

Beech

A dark, marauding secret has stalked me
all my life.
An unspeakable monster of twisted, contorted
shapes, movement and sounds.
It keeps the air from entering and leaving my lungs freely.
It grips me by the throat and squeezes
in the darkness.

My executioner.
Patiently waiting for the moment of acquiescence.

It's a black hole that accompanies me with every step.
A watchful eye
reminding me of my misdemeanours.
A magnet that I must resist and fight
constantly.

It manifests as zero tolerance of
my frailty,
my mistakes and wrong turns,
uncharitable thoughts or the odd cruel act.

Is it my purpose to be a Saint?
Am I allowed no compassion?

I can, and do, live with all of this.
I might even prosper,
metamorphose into something
beautiful or worthy.

Amongst it all there is strength and love.
Love lives here, I'm sure.
Although, it is so well hidden
I cannot find it.

Nasturtium

I feel a bit taken for granted really.
I try so hard;
Too hard?
I'm exhausted from the effort
and it's beginning to show.
Ragged looking; yellowing
and something's eating at me.
It happens every year.

I try so hard!
I shine jewel-like.
I lift my head to receive the sun.
So warm.
I'm like glowing embers.
Too hot now.
I'm thirsty and I'm irritable.
And something's eating at me still!

It's hard work holding your head up.
I feel like my neck might break.
But I have to keep trying.

Does anyone know I'm here?

An Encounter with Aconite

There's a sign that says
"Keep out!
It's worn, battered,
Cracked and cracking.
The desperate warning hardly discernible
under optimistic moss and lichen
that's hoping against hope for a
transformation;
A salvation,
A repentance
or any form of remorse.

There's a sense of decay here too.
Detritus, or possibly asphyxiation.
Can I hear wheezing?
The sound of air under pressure
pressing hard against the sides
of inlet tubes that strain
almost at breaking point.
Or perhaps it is my heart.
Loud and quickening;
pleading with me to retreat to safety.

And I am suddenly struck dumb.
Numbed with cold;
My blood freezing as our eyes meet.
And I am at once pierced through;
Impaled by vengeance;
Drowning in that purple cloak of misanthropy.

I can't tell whose anguish is the greater.
But I find myself compelled to hold this
old man who has never known a
tender touch.
My heart cracks open as his vulnerability is wrested from him
and I know truly what it means to be alone.
And I wonder what happened all those years ago
that led you to choose this life of
isolation;
Of exile.
Was there no other way?

This compassionate reverie is halted
as I realise it has gone
unnoticed,
unwanted
and I turn and run
lest my heart stops beating forever.

Jigsaw

I am a jigsaw.
I've found all the pieces.
Seemingly random shapes.
Some a little misshapen
but still holding together.
Just.

The picture is forming
but there's a section alluding me.
Each time I confront it
a grey mist descends
and none of it makes any sense.

I know there is one piece
that I'm searching for;
Hiding away in the box of my heart.
When I find it
all threads will be weaved,
all connections wired solid
and I will feel

Balanced,
Connected,
Integrated
And Whole.

Just one little piece
in the box of my Soul.

A Grieving Heart

Drowning

I used to smile when I saw droplets of dew
glistening in spiders' webs
that seemed to float and hover
over and amongst the meadow grasses.
I used to think they looked like diamonds;
A girl's best friend.

Now, they are shards of razor-sharp glass
piercing my unprotected, broken heart.
They are mirrors reflecting back a ghost;
A version of myself that I don't recognise as me.
They are a tsunami of tears
and I am drowning.

Honeysuckle

Would it be a betrayal if I left you behind?
I will still think of you
    every day.
I will still hold you in my heart;
Your love fuelling my blood; my cells,
keeping me upright.

But, my love, I need to grow.
It's time to lift my head;
    To breathe;
Create a life where the future
is untethered.

I want to feel warm again;
To feed my soul with colour
    Boldly bright.
To leave behind the grey and black.
It's time for fuschia pink, for cherry red, for royal blue

I miss the person I used to be.
I want to look in the mirror and see
    a smile;
To stretch cat-like luxuriating in the
way my body moves.

But I feel guilty at the thought
of feeling joy without you here
    beside me.
The key that would release me from this cell
is in the door
but I can't bring myself to turn it.

Will I Survive This?

It's not easy to abandon yourself
to the truth of how you really feel.
Will I ever come back to myself?
Will I survive this?

I so desperately want to remember you.
Your voice, your nose,
the way you smiled at me.
But I'm afraid to feel the intense
nothingness;
Of being hollowed out and drifting
with no sense of self.

I yearn to connect with memories
of days we shared.
To know the bond of trust and love was real
and survived the horror at the end.
How can I doubt that?

I know I must go to that dark place
and surrender to whatever I find.
I will not know peace until I do.

I will weave a net of shimmering silver thread;
Strong and secure
and cast it out before me
to be caught and held in safety
when I step into the blackness.

I will wrap my heart in your love.
A balm to soothe and shield me
when the waves of pain bear down
relentless.

I will send a root down into the earth
to anchor me steady, steadfast;
Taking in the nourishment I need
so that I can stand strong.

I will find you
and allow myself to know the truth
of how I feel.
And I will find myself
knowing I am loved and will be loved forever.

HEART BALM BY JO DYER

I Still Dream of You

I still walk toward you
with excited anticipation,
breathing in so deeply
as if this were my first breath.

I still turn the key in your door;
feeling my shoulders drop and
my jaw unlock
as I step into the sanctuary that is you.

I still sit by your fire
gazing meditatively into the heat;
Losing myself in the restorative
quiet
of the cocoon that is you.

The nights I spent curled up in your arms
gave me the most nurturing sleep of my life.
Your more than dark darkness
mirrored my own
and I found peace in it.

I still gently touch the stone walls
with outstretched fingertips
eager to receive their affirmation.
I feel the cobbled paths through my boots
on walks taken along narrow lanes;
my bones aching for you.

I walked away.
And each step hauled the anchor up
One. More. Notch.
I felt the earth fall away from me;
and forcing my head to turn
for one last look,
through burning tears, I knew I would not return.

But return I do.
In dreams so full of longing
that my heart is torn and shredded
over and over and over.
I left you.
But not quite.
Were I to return to you,
I would find my Soul behind the locked door.

It is yours to keep.

Better Days

Better days are coming;
As sure as night follows day
and day follows night.
I know this to be true.

I smell it in the black slime of January.
Something is stirring.
Somewhere deep within the unpromising sludge
old souls re-awaken – renewed
and new life takes its first breath.

I feel it in the tingle of the crisp-chilled air
as it creeps between pine trees
releasing the cleansing assurances
of its resinous gifts.

I see it in the sparkles of bright yellow,
shining, sunshine splinters
fissured by branches
still leafless,
Waiting.

I sense it in the crystal purity
of the flowing stream
where I sit entranced;
Enchanted by the myriad of miracles
surrounding me.

I touch it as I pass through;
My core ignited
with a passion;
A familiar yearning, I now recognise
as a home-coming.

And peace descends.
My heart is stilled;
I am rooted, becalmed
And I am whole again.

A Courageous Heart

I Have Drawn My Lines

I have drawn my lines
    Deep.
There will be no crossing.

Each inhalation fills my body with
    Resolve.

With each long exhalation, I am releasing
    Doubt.

Witness as I sign this pledge and I
    Rise.

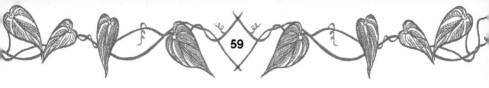
Sunday School

I see through the flimsy veil of
your lies.
I know your game.

How dare you try to frighten and
control me;
Crush my rebel spirit;
That delinquent I never knew was there,
with tales of sin and guilt and shame.

I've looked into your eyes and
I see fear
and I will not follow you.
This is not my path.

The light that guides
my way
illuminates the possibilities inherent of enquiry
and adventure.
Not the burning laser of scrutinising accusations.

I will not cower and shrink and weep
or beg forgiveness.

As I walk away
the stars will sing a chorus of approval
and my Soul will dance.

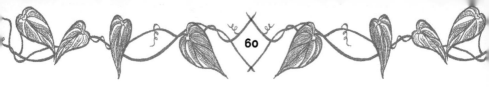

When the Day Arrives

When the day arrives
(and I know that it is coming),
I will find the courage I need
and I will be steadfast.

When the day arrives
I will not be bought,
coerced, bullied, blackmailed
or shamed into compliance.

When the day arrives
you will not find a dog
cowering in the corner whimpering
but the rabid ferocity of a She Wolf
protecting her children.

When the day arrives
I will stand in my truth
and it will illuminate and expose
your hypocrisy and lies.

When the day arrives
I *will* find the courage I need.
We will *all* find the courage we need.

Cephalaria gigantea

Is there a face beneath that shabby chic sun hat?
The wide brim guarantees anonymity.
Hastily pulled on don't you think?
As if taken by surprise.
Crept up on from behind
so that a sudden retreat into disguise was required.

Spiderman caught
vulnerable without his mask.

Still no sign of a mouth or eyes.
Is there a smile under there, or maybe tears?

Upon closer inspection shabby chic appears more like
simply shabby. Don't you agree?
She knows this.
Aah – perhaps it's shame that keeps her hidden.
Yes, that's it.
How sad. How sad.

I love my old hat.
My aged friend protecting me from scorching sun and pricking rain.
I know it looks a bit dilapidated –
well, quite a lot to tell the truth.
Seen one or two too many showers.
Yet it holds on fast,
shielding me from the piercing prods and
inquisitive glances of intrusive strangers.

The brim is far too wide
But what can you do?
It's so fabulously feminine.
Tantalisingly tousled.
Regularly random.
The resulting facelessness is a price worth paying
for the sheer joy of having it on my head.
And, it comes in useful when I venture to the village
where I know I am an object of speculation.
Or perhaps it's ridicule.
Or worse – sympathy!

What larks!
Let's keep them guessing.
I wonder at how empty their lives must be,
so fixated are they on my shortcomings.
How sad. How sad.

Watch Me

Watch me as I emerge
from my Chameleon-like existence.
Witness my feet land
on solid ground.
No more floating through life
people pleasing,
ducking and diving;
averting the disaster of discovery.

Watch me as my Daemon settles.
No more shape-shifting.
The pic n mix adjectives that defined me
are irrelevant now.
No more misunderstood,
Displaced.
Misplaced.
Not placed.

Away with the camouflaged,
Blended.
Morphing.
Hegemonic.
Seen but not acknowledged.
Heard but not listened to.

I am here; unmasked.
Shining golden;
Wings stretching in preparation.
Watch me as a take flight.

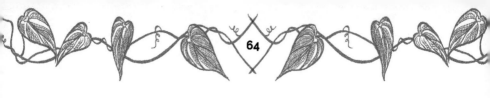

An Awakening Heart

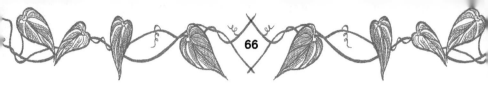

Full Moon in Scorpio

Let me take you down into the earth
where you will find such a richness
of fuel, resources and safety.

I will help you breakdown the old,
no longer needed, worn out
pieces of yourself.
Support you in shedding and discarding
the skin that no longer feels it fits.

I will help you use these parts of you
to metamorphose into something
New
Different
Vital
Healthy

A version of your essential self that you are more
at home with;
More aligned to.

It's time to relinquish the attachment you have
to what has led you here.
It has served its purpose.

And now it's time for renewal.
It's time for transformation.

Come, let me take you down into the earth.

Passion Flower

Will you let me help you
delve into the secrets of the universe?
There is so much that you don't know;
Won't know;
Can't **know**
with your eyes, ears and heart closed up
like a tiny pin prick of dark matter.

I have a direct line to the Archangels.
I scan and probe relentlessly with precisely tuned antenna.
Anemone-esque filaments capture and store
repeated mistakes, achievements and atrocities over Millenia.

It's all here for you.

I'm not so good at secrets.
I think I might burst.
I'm here to tell;
Not meant to be a repository.
This stuff is for sharing.

Can we make a deal?
I'll tell you my secrets
If you promise not to keep them secret.
This stuff is for sharing.

Imagine how different things would be.
You'd be heard at last because you listen.
You'd be seen at last because you really look.
You would never feel alone again
connected to the billions of souls residing in the other worlds;
But mostly with the one that really matters;
The one that's deep within.

Yes, I am ebullient.
A little too full of myself.
Arrogant even.
But I think you would be too if you knew what I know.

Come closer
This stuff is for sharing.

There is Life Here Afterall

It's hard to believe there is any life here.
All there is, is darkness;
An oppressive, suffocating blackness.
No sky.
No horizon.
It is dizzy-making
and I must kneel on all fours
so that I know which way up
I am.

I'm crawling like a wounded dog
whose hind legs have forsaken him.
Perhaps it is my time to die.
How I came here
I do not know.
I have no recollection of the journey.

I have landed here;
been deposited here.
A punishment perhaps,
although it is possible that I contrived it
for myself
blindly ignoring the signs
with arrogance and wrong thinking.

The choice is clear.
Crawl on in desperate hope
or embrace oblivion.
A merciful end.

But wait.
If I brought myself to this pitiful place
then surely, I can engineer
my escape;
A map or guide to navigate my way?

Straight ahead!
In the distance – a pinprick of light?
Is that a lantern?
The most precious jewel I have ever seen.
Diamond-like and glowing.
Glowing, Growing.
Closer
Closer now.

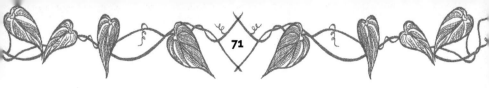

The unseen, silent hand of spirit
has not abandoned me.
I am worthy of the air that fills my lungs.
My heart will keep on pumping
rich, red blood
through my veins.
I see you.
I hear you.
There is life here after all;
My own.

Greening and Growing

As I embrace and offer up myself
to the energy of this New Moon,
I sit in awe and marvel at this
wondrous world.

As I plant new seeds in hope and expectancy,
I surrender myself and sink into
the deep stillness;
Into the ease and natural rhythm of life.

In this time of greening and growing;
Of expansion and possibility,
I cherish the instinctive chatter of birdsong.
I breathe in the fragrant Bluebells -
such a balm for the heart.
Barefoot on the grass and mossy cushions
I connect the green carpet upon which I tread
to the emerald vibrancy of my heart
and allow the two to mingle,
until I am filled with gratitude
and the perfect serenity of the moment
melts all cares away.

Now my hopes and dreams will thrive and
grow.
Robust, resilient.
To become what they are meant to be
and I will give a prayer of thankfulness
to the unseen hand that guides me.

HEART BALM BY JO DYER

New Moon in Gemini

Are you listening?
I wonder if you're ready
To have this conversation?

It's time for us to make ourselves comfortable;
Maybe with a glass of our favourite tipple
in our favourite chairs and have
a heart to heart.
How are things in your worlds?
Would you like to hear about mine?

As we share our conspiratorial tete a tete,
your airy wisdom and silky charm
coax my deepest secrets from me
out into the light.
Revealing themselves;
Delighting and possibly even surprising me.

Wrapped in your Mercurial wings,
I soar on flights of fantasy
discovering those places deep within
where I can truly know what my heart yearns for.

I'm so grateful for your willing ear today.
My heart is soothed;
My spirits uplifted,
knowing I am a cherished child of the Universe
and blessed with so much love and abundance.

AN AWAKENING HEART

I Know you're in There

I know you're in there.
I've caught the occasional glimpse
when I've ventured toward a mirror
or a window pane.

You look so very far away.
And there are veils of shimmering
chiffon, voile and damask
between us.

Miles of paths grown virtually impassable
with the promise of prickles and stings
and stubbed toes on debris.
But I can still see you;
Sense you.
You're not so far from me that you're a
total Stranger.

I have not been abandoned.

I want you to step toward me.
Could you do that for me please?
I need to see your face more clearly
so that I can confirm your identity.

I have not been abandoned.

I recognise that purposeful walk;
That jaw set with determination,
Those strong arms.
I remember the devastation this whirlwind leaves behind.
Swirling, circling,
Rising up and tossing lesser mortals
to the ground.

I feel her pulse; her drive.
I can hear her now.
Walk towards *me* she calls
Join me over here.
I know the way and we must travel together.

We have not been abandoned.

A Peaceful Heart

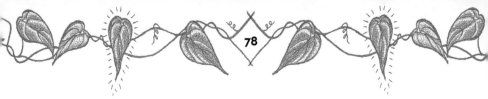
Bluebell

Poor Bluebell.
She looks so forlorn and sad;
Head drooping forward
as if all hope is gone.

I thought I heard her weeping.
I'm sure a quiet, private sob
wafted past me on the breeze.

So slender,
So delicate.
It must be exhaustion
from the effort of keeping upright.

Although it might be loneliness.
She is, after all, the only one of her kind
here.
No, I think it must be a broken heart
that lays her so low.
The grief of losing so many loved ones
or the pain of abandonment or
rejection.

Poor sad Bluebell.
Is there nothing we can do to console her?

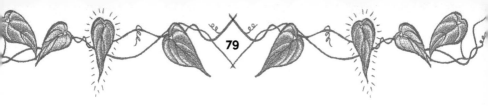
Dear friends and flowers of the meadow
please do not concern yourselves.
I merely bow my head in devotion
to the wondrous power that has brought us all
here.
Together in this glorious community of kindred Souls.

I do not weep.
Why would I?
I know and trust that I am loved
and there is no greater source of solace and strength.

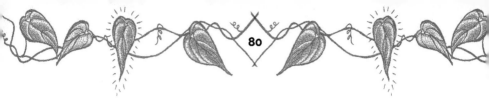

Elm

Today, I watch the clouds shapeshifting.
Floating, morphing playfully.
A flotilla of fluffiness.
Shades of grey, violet and pink.
I imagine myself ascending to join them;
Joyfully released from gravity and anchored roots.
But check myself
remembering that it will come soon anyway.
Not of my choosing.
I have found no sign of it this morning.

Today, I revel in the way the breeze
produces such a melody with my leaves.
I am music.
I sing beside the wren who rests upon my bough.
My heart soars with the Buzzards;
their gliding forms closer to heaven than I can ever hope to get.
And I have found no sign of it this morning.

Today, I watch the Kestrel hover then dip and dive.
I watch the Heron waiting;
Patience personified.
I commune with the beetles who reside within the crevices of my skin,
Comforted to know that they will have shelter
for many moons when I am gone.
But I found no sign of it this morning.

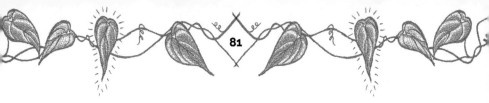
I am alone here.
Not one of my kind remains.
I stand amongst ghosts,
Some of whom I knew as friends.
Others, lost long before my time.
I have learned to be mindful; present.
Each day a gift, a blessing.
I have found no sign of it this morning.

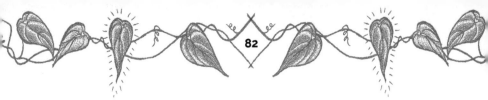

Sleeping with Mr Curry

Have you ever slept beside a man
you weren't in love with?
Didn't even like that much,
if you're honest.

I need to tell you about Mr Curry.
Do you have the stomach for a confession?

I was nervous as I approached him.
We had met several years before
and it hadn't been pretty.
You might say we had "previous".
No romantic liaison then;
Animosity.
In fact, you might label it as loathing
on my part.
Not my finest hour.

Nose wriggling in disgust –
"isn't it time you took a bath?
I can hardly breathe.
Your stench sets off my asthma!
Pick yourself up and stop molesting
those pretty young things
too polite or stupid to shrug you off.
Do they really need your embarrassing overtures
so badly?
For goodness sake, tone it down!
Must you always be the centre of attention?

That's how it was.

Until, by chance we
stumbled upon each other again.
Older and wiser maybe.
Definitely the former.

I fancied he'd want revenge.
I prepared for harsh words or perhaps
humiliation.

But as I heard his first uttering I wept;
"I forgive you", he whispered
ever so gently,
Like a caress on my cheek
wiping away tears.
"Come, let's start again.
This time look more closely.
Consider the detail.
Go beneath into the depths.
Cast your eye over every nuance.

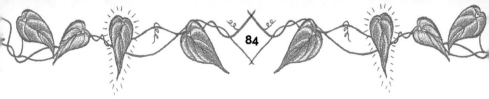

Can't you see that I am made of
golden goblets of sunshine?
A sacred chalice;
A holy grail of tenderness, tolerance, compassion?

Come lie with me
and we can right the wrongs
and soothe the pains".

And so, I did.

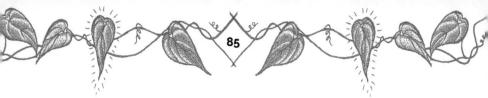

One Evening in Dorset

She came over to me
disrupting her evening reverie
to do so.
I thanked her, honoured by her gesture;
Feeling humbled that she had chosen me.

She flinched at my clumsy advances.
Too eager, too impatient, too needy
for connection.
I felt the sting of shame and regret
and apologised for my mistake;
Afraid that the moment had been lost.

But she stayed
and rested her gaze upon me.
And I responded likewise.
Only a few seconds were needed until
we were quieted in a deep and sacred stillness;
Until I felt her heart open to me
and mine to hers.

I reached out my hand
and gently brushed away some flies bothering her eyes
as tenderly as was possible.
Her eyelashes were soft and silken.
Then we stood,
my cheek against her warm face
breathing each other in
each of us stilled and gentled by the other.

The world disappeared.
There was just us two
held in a tender trance
of love and trust.

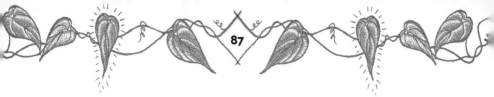
The Gorgeousness of Fog

Does the fog call to you?
Coax you from the familiar, every day, mundane?
Can you resist opening the door and stepping into the parallel universe
    waiting for you?
Entering into compulsory circumspection,
An enforced 'nowness' as there is no 'other'?
Will you revel in the muffled, swirling, eeriness?
Where each movement is a leap of faith;
All senses strained and heightened as you become
    as a ghost
walking through walls
Thrusting your hands from one universe to another
Unseen, unknown?
Is your breath in your throat, your head or your chest?
It's hard to tell but it makes a different sound.
Is your heart beating faster? Will it stop?
    Just like that?
Can you let the fog take you;
Let your limbs dissipate, your heart unfurl itself,
All boundaries dissolve and
Let the gorgeousness of fog claim you?

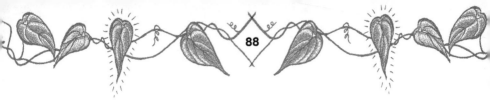

Cephalaria Bud

I want you to know that
the perfection you seek
is an illusion.
You know this
and yet you still yearn for it
as if, through your longing or
by sacrificing yourself to its Gods and Goddesses
it can be magicked into existence.

I want you to know that
even though my petals burst forth randomly
in apparent chaos
from my mathematically precise buds,
all is as it is meant to be.
There is no need for alarm.
And I'm curious as to why your nose
wriggles your disapproval of my perceived misdemeanours.

I want you to know that
there will be a time when
the anarchy of my unveiling will not trouble you.
You will know with the certainty of your own mortality
that each petal is unleashed
when the time is right
so that the unfurling comes with ease
and creates the most exquisitely imperfect whole
upon which the Bees will feast.

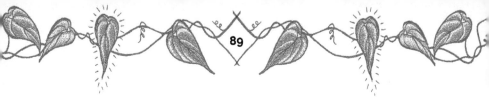

So, This Is What Freedom Feels Like

And so, she dared to look back
along the stretched-out corridor she had
travelled.
Like a runway
with door, upon door, upon door
that had been unlocked and opened.
Some with trepidation,
Others with giddy anticipation.
And she smiled.

She pressed on,
Heart thumping and pounding
in her chest.
Knowing that soon she would be
invited to open yet another.
Feeling suddenly tired at the imagined
effort it would take to move it
Just. One. Inch.
And she sighed.

But as she approached,
she found the door already open
and she was running fast toward it
and was through in
a second;
Gasping and in awe as
she tried to take in what was
laid out before her.

Such an expanse of blue sky.
An armada of fluffy clouds;
A breeze caressing her cheeks;
No land beneath her feet!

Flying!
Flying through the air!
As naturally as breathing.
She dipped and dived
Bird-like.
Acrobatically dancing;
The joy of it filling her heart.

So, this is what freedom feels like
She laughed.

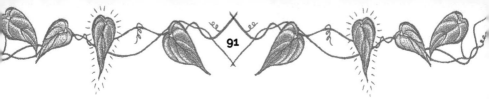

Home-Coming

Rest awhile and allow
the warmth to comfort you.
Hold up your face and arms
and stretch up your torso
so that the light can enter every pore,
every muscle fibre,
every cell.

Sit awhile and watch
golden sparkles dance and play
upon the surface of water.
Let yourself become a light-filled,
shimmering, glowing piece of dust
that is blown flying,
sent whooshing over hills and mountains,
lakes and valleys.

Before resting once again
upon the grass
where you kiss the daisies
tenderly,
delighted at your home-coming.

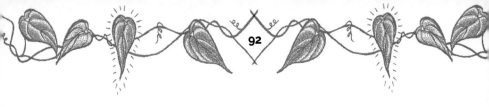

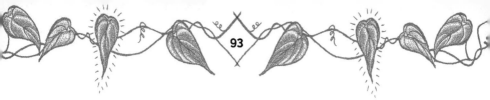

A Match Made in Heaven

When I first thought of writing this book, I imagined it would simply be a collection of poems. But, like the universe, the book had other ideas and as I came toward the end of the writing and compilation, it presented me with the suggestion that we should include a final section where I listed vibrational essences that would help each of the emotional qualities of the heart featured in the different sections of the book. After all, it said, you have often said that Vibrational Essences and Poetry are a match made in heaven. So, for example, if someone reading the poems resonated strongly with and felt the pain of a lonely heart, which vibrational essences might help them to shift their energetic state and enable them to find themselves again and feel less alone and isolated?

How could I refuse the wisdom of this book whose own essence has been my companion and guide for so many years? So, I have chosen one poem from each section and suggested several essences from different essence ranges that will support anyone seeking support in such situations.

I hope you'll agree that this is fitting way to end the book. It's strange (or maybe it isn't), how these things develop.

So, as I said, it was never my intention when I started out to write this book to produce something 'about' vibrational essences. That was the furthest thing from my mind. In fact, when I scribbled the first of the poems into my notebooks I had only scant knowledge of the Bach Essences. I knew nothing of the Lightbringer, Alaskan, Australian Bush, FES essences and the like. I'd used Bach essences for myself for many years but my experience and understanding were limited to the handful that I used

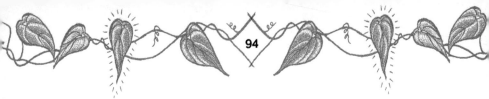
regularly. The possibility of becoming an essence practitioner was the Universe's best kept secret to be revealed to me when the time was right.

Initially, it was the connection, love and empathy I had developed for nature as a professional gardener that led me to start writing these poems. I had always loved flowers since childhood and I became curious and wanted to know more of how they experienced the world; what it is like to be a Beech or Elm tree, a Rose or a Nasturtium. I spent my gardening days with them, immersed in their energy and I listened and these poems (some of them), are what I heard.

I find it rather lovely that the reason I chose to do the course that led me to becoming an essence practitioner was a desire to connect more deeply with the flowers and with nature so that I could write these poems. I wanted to experience them differently and deeply. It is also rather lovely that since I decided to become an essence practitioner, they have spoken to me more loudly and with more potency.

So, with all that in mind, here we go. Please bear in mind that there are many suitable essences for each emotional state – these are just a few suggestions.

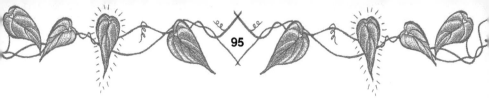
A Bruised Heart

Let's start with A Bruised Heart and for this, I have chosen **Mr Pendulus Beech**.

I am totally in love with Mr Pendulus Beech. He is a real tree growing in Belper Cemetery, close to my home. I find it tragic that he lives in his brother's shadow; comparing himself unfavourably; adopting a 'victim' mentality. He has forgotten that he has his own wonderful gifts and unique and precious essence to offer us. Yes, he has suffered – there are far too many calloused wounds where the chainsaw has left its mark – but he has forgotten that he can choose how to 'be'. He has chosen blame and bitterness. "I could've been magnificent too" – he chooses not to see his own magnificence; he has forgotten how to be grateful. He has closed his heart to happiness.

The Essences I would suggest to him are:

Bach Essences:

Holly to open his heart and bring about a shift in perspective towards a more generous and loving disposition – especially towards himself and his brother.

Willow for the part of his personality that blames others and takes no responsibility for his circumstances, choosing resentment and bitterness instead.

Pine for his feelings of low self-worth and low-self esteem.

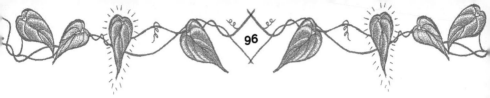
Crab Apple for his feelings of self-loathing.

Alaskan Essences – Gold for the tendency to compare himself to others and for not recognising and valuing his own gifts. Essentially this is about self-acceptance.

Lightbringer Essences: Chickweed Wintergreen to help him show himself compassion; to help with his guilt and shame.

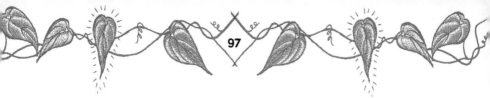
The Angry Heart

The Angry Heart can present with many difficult and complex emotions. It's not always obvious that anger is at the root of a person's distress. In this section, there is one poem that displays the pain and complexity of anger well – this is **Holly**.

> "Today, my veins pulsate with a stalking anger that
> Frightens me.
> My spikes are not for my protection but for yours".

Fortunately, there are a lot of essences available to us for anger – but it's also important to ascertain the story behind the anger – it comes in so many colours and hues.

The Essences I would suggest are:

Bach Essences:

Holly – as described above.

Beech – An essence for intolerance – of others but also of our own flaws. Beech helps us to see the world with more compassion (and that includes ourselves).

Clematis – to bring a grounding energy. To bring the person back to themselves.

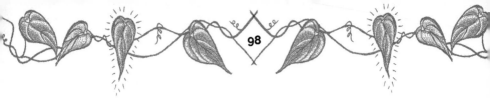
Cherry Plum – in this poem there is an edge that it seems this individual may step across at any moment. Cherry Plum is the essence for when you feel you might 'lose it'.

Lightbringer Essences:

Vipers Bugloss – A useful essence for when you are prone to blurt out harsh words that wound – Vipers Bugloss helps us to bite our tongue and use our words more wisely.

Hare's Foot Clover – helps you to release prickly behaviour and defensiveness or if in another person, helps you not to rise to it or be triggered by them.

Birch Fire – to help you to stand in the energy of your anger, staying peaceful and calm despite the rage inside. A 'diffusing' essence that helps to calm a situation so that it doesn't get out of hand.

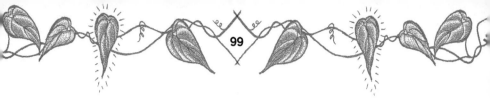

The Lonely Heart

For the Lonely Heart I have chosen the poem **Rose**. I've always thought that this Rose is trapped in a time capsule, unable to move on. Her existence seems very sterile and empty. She seems to endure life rather than live it. This Rose grew in the garden of my previous home.

"She sits upright in delicate shades of pink silk and cashmere.
Soft, quivering colours and textures
Disguising steeliness, resilience
and a tendency towards hostility".

The Essences I would suggest:

Bach Essences:

Water Violet for people who feel isolated and alone – mainly because of a deep sense of alienation from the self.

Holly – to open up the heart chakra,

Honeysuckle – to help her to move forward and leave the past behind,

Rock Water – to help her to be more spontaneous, less rigid and attached to her 'regimes'.

Lightbringer Essences:

Bluebell – for her broken heart. It helps us to trust in love again.

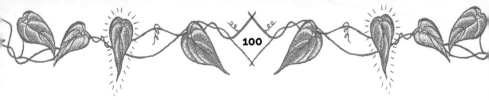

Heart Balm combination – to soothe the heart when it feels cold and sad, to radiate loving energy from the heart and to support our ability to give and receive love.

Pink Frangipani – Also about receiving an giving love due to the a lack of self-worth.

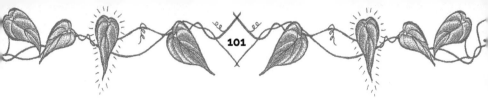

A Grieving Heart

From the section A Grieving Heart I've chosen the poem *Honeysuckle*. This is a poem for the later stages of grief where the heart is in a dilemma. It is ready to move on; to begin a new life – but not quite. Moving out into the world again raises many questions and emotions – guilt and fear of judgement to name just two.

> "But I feel guilty at the thought
> of feeling joy without you here
>   beside me.
> The key that would release me from this cell
> is in the door
> but I can't bring myself to turn it".

The Essences I would Suggest:

Bach Essences:

Honeysuckle – helps to look forward rather than over one's shoulder. It is an essence for letting go of the things that no longer serve us. Grief is a necessary process. It is a healing process but when it is complete, it is time to leave it behind. Honeysuckle helps us to do just that.

Pine – helps with feelings of guilt.

Walnut – helps to process the changes in our circumstances and also to stay centred and balanced if others do challenge us.

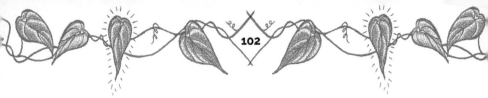
Rescue Remedy – This is a combination of 5 essences to help you become calm and present again when you have a wobble or acute feelings of distress. When the waves of grief hit – this is the essence to reach for.

Lightbringer Essences:

Ruby-in-the-Storm – An essence to help you in extreme circumstances of despair, grief and stress

Scots Primrose – helps you to stay in the loving energy of your heart so that you can 'be' with difficult circumstances.

Cotton Grass – An essence to help with shock and trauma. Provides a safe haven when you are feeling distress.

Alpine-Forget-Me-Not – An essence for when we feel abandoned by Source, God, The universe – whatever you call it. To help us know again that we will always be loved and that love does not die – we will always be connected to our loved ones through source and our heart.

Light Support Combination – fulfils a similar role to rescue remedy

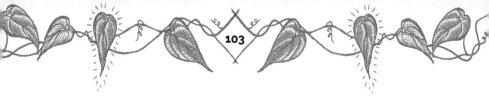

A Courageous Heart

The next section is A Courageous Heart and I've chosen **When the Day Arrives** as the poem to discuss here. This poem was written as a word potion for a client. It is a poem that speaks of the need to be resilient in the face of profound challenges, anger at a situation that has been forced upon them, the fear felt as a result of the knowledge that there is a battle approaching.

> "When the day arrives
> you will not find a dog
> cowering in the corner whimpering
> but the rabid ferocity of a She Wolf
> protecting her children".

The Essences I would suggest are:

Bach Essences:

Mimulus – for courage

Larch – for confidence and self belief

Agrimony – to help with speaking up – voicing your opinions and needs

Holly – for anger, keeping your heart chakra open.

Lightbringer essences:

Grass of Parnassus – for standing in your truth and power.

Scots Pine Combination – for being steadfast and strong when in challenging and difficult circumstances

Ruby-in-the-Storm. See grief above.

Northern Marsh Orchid – An emboldening essence that helps us to stand up to those who would try to intimidate or bully us

Moon Magic Essences (My own essences)

Full Moon in Aquarius – This is an essence of resilience, courage and steadfastness. It's an essence to take when you have any kind of battle on your hands. It's also an essence for collective action – perhaps when you're fighting authority. It's very much about collaboration, the comfort of strangers and the strength of the collective. An essence for the difficulties that humankind is facing all over the world.

New Moon in Virgo – an essence for when you feel like you're in peril – not feeling safe – but more than this, feeling a sense of loss and sadness at the same time.

An essence to take when the state of the world and the worst of human nature becomes too much.

Full Moon in Leo – Provides a source of strength and support – knowing that you have a centre of wisdom and peace to go to whenever you need it

The Awakening Heart

The Awakening Heart is a heart becoming more aware of what it needs to live a contented, fully expressed life. There are so many essences that could be helpful here. We are all awakening in ways unique to ourselves and our Soul's purpose so I'm finding it hard to choose essences for this section.

There are two poems in this section that were written as a direct result of making essences – they describe the essence qualities and something of the experience of making the essences so I have written about those. These are **Passion Flower** and **There is Life Here Afterall.**

The Awakening Heart needs to tune into the signs and messages it is getting from the Universe and to listen to itself and trust its intuition. This is what the **Passion Flower Essence** is all about.

Passion Flower is an essence that helps you to listen. It helps you to connect with your deepest knowing, to your higher self and to the Universe. I like to describe it as having a satellite array wired to your Soul.

The poem There is Life Here Afterall describes what I saw and felt when I co-created the moon essence, **New Moon in Aquarius**. It was the first Moon Essence I made in January 2020.

This essence helps the Awakening Heart because it helps us to TRUST the universe. The universe will always be our guiding light; it will always be there for us. This essence helps us to deeply trust that the universe is giving us what we need to grow – not necessarily what we want.

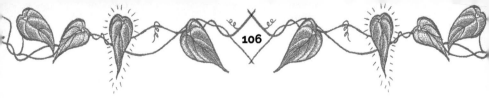
"The unseen, silent hand of spirit
has not abandoned me.
I am worthy of the air that fills my lungs.
My heart will keep on pumping
rich, red blood
through my veins".

The Peaceful Heart

Finally, the Peaceful Heart – does this Heart need vibrational essences? Perhaps less so. Perhaps only occasionally but there are essences that will help us to maintain this easeful way of living. We may need support to stay balanced, open hearted, serene and living from our heart with love.

The poems that remind me of this are *Home Coming* and *Cephalaria Bud*. There are two Lightbringer Essences that I feel are perfectly suited to aid the energy of Home Coming and these are **Serenity and Linden Blossom. Serenity** is an essence of calm and stillness; perfect for helping meditation and mindfulness. **Linden Blossom** is an essence of light-heartedness and joy.

Another essence that I have found to be particularly helpful in maintaining an optimistic lightness of being is my **New Moon in Aries** essence. This is an essence with a 'Can Do' energy, optimistic, light and enthusiastic. Whenever I take it, I just feel 'better'. I am less worried, less concerned, less burdened. Not that I walk around anxious, worried, burdened all the time – no, I don't. But this essence just brings about an 'ease' to life. It's one of my favourite essences.

Cephalaria Bud is an essence that I made from the *Cephalaria gigantea* buds. This poem describes the message it has for us and I feel it has a role to play in maintaining the peaceful heart because it warns of striving for perfection and control when these things are illusions that simply lead to dis-ease. Cephalaria Bud reminds us that everything is unfurling just as it is meant to. The way to a peaceful heart is to let go – ALLOW life to unfurl; allow yourself to be surprised and delighted at the unexpected adventures it throws at you.

"Let yourself become a light-filled,
shimmering, glowing piece of dust
that is blown flying,
sent whooshing over hills and mountains,
lakes and valleys.

Before resting once again
upon the grass
where you kiss the daisies
tenderly,
delighted at your home-coming".

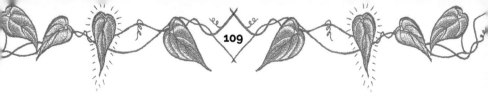

Acknowledgements and Gratitude

would like to express my sincere gratitude to my clients who have inspired the Word Potions that appear in this book and for their permission to use them.

I would also like to offer my heartfelt thanks to my mentor and teacher, Mary Weaver and The Universe for guiding me to co-create essences with Moon energy. Mary knew exactly what she was doing when she asked me the innocent question "Can you make essences with the Moon?". You have really started something, Mary – which was, of course, your intention. I love you for it.

A very special thanks goes to Emily Nature – the Book Doula – who has walked this path with me for almost a year and has helped me in so many ways to bring this book into being. Your beautiful energy and skills as a coach have brought me here so much quicker than I imagined. Thank you so much.

Thanks too to Val Gilman of Tap Root Art and Design who has guided me to believe in myself as an artist and writer of poems. Your coaching and co-working sessions have led to some of the poems in this book and I will be forever grateful for your friendship and tender coaching skills. Thanks too to my co-working artists – Michelle, Carol, Noah and Emet for the wonderful witnessing you shared during our time together.

I am so grateful to Emet Aron for the wonderful drawings of Mr Pendulus Beech and the Heart Balm Vine that adorn the pages of this book. I'm looking forward to more projects with you.

Thanks go to Gayle Johnson and the WordSpill writers and to Vishwam Heckert and Amara George Parker who inspire me to find opening lines and routes in to the poems.

I also want to thank Rachel Singleton of Lightbringer Essences, firstly for creating such a beautiful range of essences and secondly for her generous heart in agreeing for me to call the book Heart Balm. Heart Balm is one of Rachel's wonderful essence combinations and is truly a beautiful gift. Thank you so much Rachel for everything you do.

Thank you Sam Pearce of SWATT Books who took my manuscript and turned it into this book. You are worth your weight in gold.

Thanks go to my partner, Chris, who has patiently listened to me drone on about where each poem should go, what font I prefer, how to use the drawings, whether I should produce a hardback etc etc. You are my rock and I'm so very grateful but I can't promise your ordeal is over.

Finally, my love and gratitude are boundless for the whispers of the trees, flowers, animals, and moons that have inspired the co-creation of these poems. I love you with all my heart and hope you will continue to whisper your magic to me.

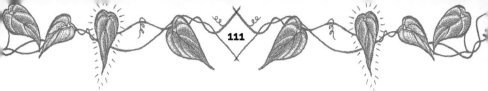

About the Author

Heart Balm is Jo's first collection of poems and is primarily inspired by the flowers and trees which she has loved since she was a small child. She started her professional life as a researcher and lecturer in the University sector but soon found herself searching for something else. She discovered flower essences and 'energy work' in her early thirties and trained in therapeutic and Thai massage. She eventually found her way to horticulture and re-trained to became a professional gardener at the age of 42.

It was during the time she spent working as a head gardener that she first became aware of the whispers of the flowers and her growing sensitivity to them. She realised that an even deeper connection was needed if she was to succeed in writing the poems that she knew the flowers and her Soul wanted her to write and this led her to embark on a practitioner level course in flower and vibrational essences (she had been using flower essences for herself for thirty years). She became a qualified practitioner in 2019 and now combines essences and 'word potions' to help her clients embody deeply transformational energetic shifts so that they say YES to life.

Jo is still a keen gardener and volunteers at a local park where she is helping to create a wildlife garden. She loves to go walking in the woodlands and over the hills in Derbyshire where she lives with her partner and their cat, Eddie.

You can find out more about Jo and her work here: www.jodyer.co.uk or www.facebook.com/essencewithjodyer